ROOM 5608

HALEY MACLEOD

ISBN: 0995999902
ISBN-13: 978-0-9959999-0-9

I dedicate this book to
every soul
paralyzed with pain
yet love is a crave
the heart still seeks

to taste
to touch
to know

CONTENTS

when poetry finds you
brutality begins to feel a lot like
healing
she enters into the hallway
of your heart gently
you can hear her singing the demons to sleep
for your ribcage no longer
has room to carry all the darkness
they brought to you
it is time you learn how to *gently*
carry your own weight

when poetry finds you
she brings roses to your cemetery
breathing solace
over the parts of you that have
died
so you can finally let go
of what makes you feel everything but
alive
with sunlight dripping from her hands
she puts the entire
universe
back into your soul
sewing your brokenness with the light
of every fallen star in the galaxy
so you can finally realize
all of this hurt is temporary
you will shed this skin
when the gods call you to come back home

poetry comes to teach you a purpose
she gives you a pen and whispers

write until you see
the wisdom birthing from all your pain
write until you feel
you are stronger than your pain
write until it is the pain
that brings you back home

GENESIS

please do not listen
to my stories of the wars
and cry
i have spent far too many years
draining myself into oceans
instead come sing survival
with me

POETRY

DEPARTURE

tell me about departure – what does it feel like?

the weight of the world pressing against
your chest
emptiness penetrating the walls of your lungs
thinning the air of your memory
constant panic floods your veins
knowing you will always be missing something
a limb
your heart
the light
him
waking up to a sunless day
falling asleep under a sky without the moon
departure breaks in without warning
causing a forest fire of havoc
to tear apart the years of love
you built with someone
burning down every place
every moment you ever called home
departure happens so quickly
you cannot catch it with your hands
or speak your words fast enough
it leaves you to drown
a thousand excruciating deaths
breaking you more and more
every single time

you start to think of all the things you wish
you could say
but you know it is too late
it is too late
you watch the sand of the hourglass pile
higher and higher inside of your soul
slowly slipping further and further
into a galaxy of oblivion
an eternity of misery
while your hands are still trying to hold on
you cannot find the strength to let go
you do not want to let go

for the first time your body begins
to familiarize with the term
collapsing
you never knew fear and heartbreak
could flood your veins
this deeply
like the aftermath of a hurricane
when everything is destroyed
departure is the consuming heaviness that
stays
after everything
leaves
it will always stay

you will go on to live the rest of your life
haunted
every time the phone rings
every time someone says your name
you will cry
in the softest
most catastrophic way
writing letters to your past
hoping everything
everyone
the hands of departure took
knows how much it hurt without them then
and how much it still hurts without them now
it will never stop hurting

departure
calls to take something away even
if that means
it takes you away too

THE BRAVEST DAY YOU WILL LIVE

you are gone
yet the war of you
has never left

you set me on fire
so i would burn
the way you did
so i would always carry pain
the way you did
so i would suffer
underneath the same bleeding sky
the way you did
so my scars would always look
the way yours did

HISTORY

instead of bringing the water here to
cleanse me
you turned the faucet
jammed the plug
nailed me to the bathtub
silently watched horror
flood my lungs
drowning me

that was the day
you hung me by my heart
for showing you my vulnerability

MOTHER KNOWS BEST

i am a spinning image
of everything that ever loved you
and destroyed you

i am nothing but a sad reminder
of the sorrow that still lives in your bones
from everything that has ever left you

you never liked the colour of my eyes
when i looked at you
you never saw me
all you could ever see
were the shades of
him

APOLOGIZING FOR WEARING THE FLESH OF MY FATHER

when i think of you
i cannot escape the trauma
that begins to seep out of my pores
all i hear is the sound
of a thousand doors slamming
i carry the burden
of your departure
behind my swollen eyes
i shed enough tears
to drown a thousand times
for death is something my heart
knows once more

who taught you how to only spit fire
when you say the word
goodbye
who showed you only how to
walk out the door
and never come back
what kind of monster lives inside you
that makes you forget
you were the womb
that once held me
it was your blood i drank
that birthed me into this world

FOSTER HOMES

my scars
found a way to speak to me
they told me

you did not leave
because
you did not love me
you left
because
you did not know
how to love yourself

DEAR MOTHER

when you would say it
my lungs would choke
on the word
hope
begging that it was not
the whiskey talking
that this time it was really you
when you would say it
the pulse in my aching heart
the bruises on my soul
the blood on my knuckles
would begin to forgive you
would begin to believe you too
when you would say it
the demons you built inside of me
would crumble
even they finally felt
the light coming through

this is how you became the prison
this is how i became the prisoner

you knew exactly how to build me
you knew exactly how to break me

DEAR FATHER

every time he said
he loved me

i have been at war
with my mind lately
trapped inside the abyss
of my subconscious
fighting a war of pandemonium
with the person i am now
and the person *i used to be*

ACCEPTANCE

i don't want to feel
the part of me
that misses you
anymore

they ask
i crumble
they speak louder
i fall apart even more

who is your mother
who is your father
who raised you
who is to thank for the kindness in your soul

(me)

i was a child reared by the hands
of two broken parents
addiction
was the blood of my father
depression
was the face of my mother
i learned the word *hate* from the mouth
of my mother every time she
spit fire speaking about a man
i learned the word *pain* from the wounds
of my father
watching him grab a bottle thinking
the whiskey will heal his scars
the whiskey will love him
back

i was a child reared by two parents
who could not find a way
to hold each other gently
without imprinting bruises on skin
i was taught
love was another word for war

don't you dare think you won't walk away
without scars
love never wins
if you believe it does then you will walk
away losing
(we all walked away losing)

i lost my father to his addictions
i lost my mother to her depression
i lost my sisters to years of silence
for we were never taught words to make
amends
all i had left
to hold onto was myself
i decided i would be the one
who never leaves

i will awake to the warmth of the sunrise
she will be my mother
i will fall asleep under the protection of
the moon
he will be my father
the earth will become my sister
bringing me fire
water
air
into my soul

i went on to raise myself
to always carry kindness in my back pocket
to study the word love
till i could feel it
running through my veins
with waters of healing

who is going to congratulate you with roses
on the day of your graduation
who is going to walk you down the aisle
on your wedding day
who is going to be there when your
first child is born
who is going to let you know how proud
they are of the woman you have become
of how much you have grown

i cannot answer any of these questions
without my entire ribcage caving
i cannot afford to have them know the truth
why i can't fall asleep until 3 a.m.
why anxiety has flooded my body
why every time i watch the sun rise
i cry
begging to feel the light
pour into my aching bones
and heal all this hurt buried deeply inside

so i lie
so i lie
so i lie

gently exiting the conversation with

enough about me
tell me about you
how is your mother
how is your father
is everything going ok for you
me
everyone is great
perfect
i am just fine
perfectly fine

REVERSE PSYCHOLOGY

seek balance in all you do

too much sun can burn you
too much lust can blind you
too much control can break you

i am sorry for loving you
with such intensity
such depths
that your heart
could never find a way
to hold it all
that your hands
could never find a way
to hold *all of me*

I AM STILL LEARNING HOW TO HOLD ALL OF ME

when did you lose your softness?

the day i watched the moon
(him)
walk away from the sun
(her)

the way her eyes
quietly bled dry through the night
knowing freedom was dripping
from his mouth as he was swallowing
the fire of someone else
the way her hands forgot how to hold
the way her lungs forgot how to breathe
knowing the same body
she spent years making love to
had been sleeping with the stars
that seemed to feed his soul more light

it was excruciating
watching love harden her slowly
like an open jar of honey
a rose deprived of water
a morning without the sunrise

just like the sun
the day you could no longer see my light
existing inside of the universe
of your heart at night
i lost my softness
i lost my tenderness
i lost my compassion

I LOST MYSELF LOVING YOU

my hands only knew how to give
your hands only knew how to take
the more i lay here beside desolation
the more i feel the ground
we once built our world upon
tremble
break

you only loved me
when the lights went down
with your eyes closed
while the whole entire time
i laid still
with my eyes burning

wide awake

A PARALLEL UNIVERSE

i always find myself searching for you
in the depths of the ocean
to every phase of the moon

just ask the stars
they will tell you
how many nights
i went moonless
bleeding
breaking
begging
all for you

IT WILL ALWAYS BE ALL FOR YOU

where were you
when i needed you
you were off
wanting
needing
someone else
to be honest
that hurt has never left me
that hurt pulls on the strings
of my heart
everyday

i feel when you look at me
you wish i was someone else
whoever she is
whoever they are
i hope someday
i can love someone
the way you love your
someone else

DRUXY

the worst part
was the heaviness
replacing the spaces in me
he once occupied
the silence greeting my thoughts
after the midnight hour
the emptiness seizing my bones
the bareness touching my skin
the aftermath
the withdrawals
of having love
enter my heart unexpectedly
then suddenly all at once
being gone

VACANT HEARTS

i should have known
all you wanted was
for someone to know you
i should have known
all you wanted was for someone
to stay
long enough to help you
figure yourself out
i should have known
you did not crave conversation
you wanted your depth
only to be felt
to be seen beyond
the silhouette of your skin
through every extent
of your soul's corner
to be loved
through and throughout

THE REALIZATION THAT SEEPS THROUGH WOUNDS AFTER THE FALLOUT

i emptied out the contents of my heart
just so you could see
that you existed solely in there
that nothing else ever
had permanent residency
you occupied every part of me
and now that you are gone
all i feel is
vacancy

CHECKOUT TIME

maybe it is my hands
that are selfish
for wanting to hold all of you
maybe it is my mind
that is consumed
in the way my thoughts obsess
wanting to know all of you
maybe it is only god
who knows the way
i pray for redamancy

i fear that
i need you
more than i need me

THE EXCHANGE

the hardest pill to swallow
is your name
i've been mixing memories
with amnesia
to suppress the pain
the aftermath of you feels
like asphyxiation

my lungs start to collapse
with the feel of a relapse
not even the vodka
can wash you away

TEMPORARY FIXES

he is long gone
while i remain here
drowning in the ocean
that formed the second
i fell in love with him
still trying to find the drain
to empty out the remains of his love
empty out every single
drop of him

LEAKY FAUCETS

here i am
left with these hands
stained
from trying to paint
the walls of our love
red
dripping from the strings of my heart
is all the love
you abandoned inside of me

it is time you see how
much i loved you
and how it still spills
out of me
in a thousand different ways
in a thousand different shades

STAINS OF TRYST

i want to know
where do i put all the memories
all the feelings that still linger
the stains from my heart bleeding dry
why do i feel more weight now that he's
gone
yet remain empty inside
i want to know
how to permanently numb the pain
not just quiet it
with a temporary fix

i want to know
how to get back into my skin
to **who i was**
before him
before all of this

MOVING DAY

the hardest part of it all
was trying to touch you
and having my hands turn
into quicksand
or always showing up
just as you were leaving
or saying *i love you*
to find you already wrote it
for someone else

falling in love so deeply
with the right person
just to have the clock
tell me it was
the wrong time

THE TASTE OF HIRAETH

it all happened so quickly
i could not catch it with my hands
or speak my words fast enough
there was so much more
i wanted love to be
us to be
but before we could begin
the hourglass ran out
and time whispered

it's over
it's over

THE TASTE OF GOODBYE

i feel you next to me
when my eyes are closed
i open my eyes
you are miles away

that is my heart playing tricks on my brain
that is reality waking up my dreams
that is wishing for sunlight
in the darkest cave of the world
that is how i feel
every waking day of loving you

POURING SALT ON MY OWN WOUNDS

the words of my heart
get washed down the drain of silence
all because you make me lose control
proving these walls of my body
i built of stone
reveal the truth
that maybe underneath my skin
i am still weak
for right when i wave my flag thinking
the battle is over
i realize it would take an army of me
to defeat the way i feel for you
to defeat all of this love
i have here inside of me
for you

WEAPONS OF DELUSION

you wanted love to be a shallow river
while i was already an ocean deep
you wanted love behind the shadows
while i exposed you on a marquee
your heart beat momentarily
while the love i bled for you
was forever
my heart was made to serve
yours was made to sever

FAIT ACCOMPLI

forgive me

for the way my mouth
spills out love recklessly
for the way my hands tremble
at the feel of your perplexity
for trying to colour over
all your lines of ebony
for wanting to cut off all the strings
that tangle your heart in complexity

WHAT IS LOVE WITHOUT TRAGEDY

it is bitter to kiss the lips of love
and taste parataxic distortion
to swim currents of someone's love
just to drown heavily in their ocean
to greet the hands of delusion
and to have paradoxical confusion
tell you that all along love
was just an illusion

THE STATE OF PHANTASMAGORIA

i would be the first to tell you
how your eyes bleed rays of light
that mimic the exact prisms
scattered in a rainbow
while you would be the first to tell me
how you are sick of my metaphoric mind
and the ways i find poetic justice
in between all of your lines

THE TASTE OF HIM WAS IRONY

with these mixed vibrations
i begin to question our existence
starting to get the message
no need to be passive aggressive
you hate the silence
want me to be more expressive
so i recite these poems for you
only to have you
call me obsessive
is love not supposed to be
over-the-top excessive

goes to show
we do not see the same
colour anymore
feel the same love anymore

you cannot compromise
the spectrum of your soul
to become a shade of grey
in a black and white heart
incapable of seeing your colour anyway

SOMBER AFFAIRS

we have these hungry hearts
mouths full of eager words
that ache for love to fill up our empty holes
we are born thirsty
drinking ourselves into a coma
with her love
his love
craving to consume love
from these hearts that we know
are no good for us

it is like we know
we are drinking poison
yet we cannot help
but love the way it burns
they burn

LA DOULEUR EXQUISE

tell me how it is that you are not even here
yet the shadow of your heart still remains here
haunting me

when i am with you
the pain running through my blood
turns to honey
the scars on my heart remember
what it is like to breathe
i crawl back into my
skin
wanting to be loved again
ready to let the sun pour into my brokenness
softly swallowing down the letters of
healing

when i am without you
the second you leave
my walls begin to build back up
the veins leading to my heart
constrict
conceal
my thoughts turn to quicksand
the hourglass
slowly begins to remind me
that the only time i am alive
is when i am with you
other than that
i do not know how to love
i do not know how to feel

SOUL MATES

maybe we were searching
for the same love
and along the same lines
we lost it
we were trying to alter
the chemicals of our love
the aftermath was diabolic

we had each other convinced
that mixing in pleasure
would push out any pain but
the lust made you reckless
the love made me insane

EMERGENCY EXITS

i do not want to remember
i cannot seem to forget

i travel down memory lane
covered in stains of regret
from the remains of your love
they have not left yet

you still hold the gun to my heart
in this game of russian roulette

LUST LACED BULLETS

how many apologies
until sorry is a word
left without meaning
how many tears
until you have filled an ocean
with the colour of dysphoria
how many times
will you let him break down
the castle walls you have built
why do you hold onto him
when he has a rope tied around your heart

he is draining all the love out of you
you stand there
with your own hands wrapped
around your neck
letting him

BRUISED PEACHES

you are the smoke in my lungs
leaving me gasping for air
lately i have been kissing these bottles
thinking you will be there
down at the bottom
in the emptiness of the glass
instead all i find is myself
my reflection staring back

i find myself lost somewhere
between the lie i have become
drowning in your love
it keeps me forever young
forever in thought
i crave your perfection
forever in love
you have become my perception

it is 3 a.m. and
i find myself lost
in the memory of loving you

THE TASTE OF ADDICTIONS

i do not even need to look at you
i feel the distance
i go to give you my love
all you give me back is resistance
on a level so consistent
you have embodied the means
of persistence
leaving me a closet of skeletons
just to remind me

that you
that i
and this universe of us
are all nonexistent

SUBLIMINAL MESSAGES

you were addicted to the white lines
feeding me love through your white lies
blowing smoke in my lungs
permanently high

i became your antidote
you became my kryptonite

HEADED FOR REHAB

when you feel the alcohol burning
yet it is not enough to suppress
the memories of them bleeding out of you
that are covering you in regret
when the drugs start to taste
the same as your pain
and you cannot swallow
or stomach
the letters of their name
may you realize your only true antidote
is finding the strength
to let him
to let her
go

THE LAST BREATH BEFORE
AN OVERDOSE

love never came with daggers
that was something
you brought to the table

INFIDELITY

so powerless
so restless
you have me
with my back
against the wall
defenseless
heart tied in knots
lungs breathless
screaming mercy
for the way you pour love over me
so reckless

BREATHING UNDERWATER

just when i go to erase you out of me
i remember how you exist
dancing around the corners of my eyelids
painted underneath all my memories

i cannot forget you
how can i forget you
when our brain
serves the purpose
of helping us remember

THE TASTE OF TRAUMA

you left an ocean of
melancholy
inside me
the second your tongue
spoke of her
as your remedy
and me
as your tragedy

INCREDULITY

when they rip your heart out of your
chest
do not fight like hell to get it back
you gave it to them
when you wrote forever upon their lips

let them have it
for it will bleed out
nothing but memories
let them keep the one thing
that makes you hold on
that way you can
finally
move on

A HEART TRANSPLANT

how can i put out this fire of love
when the flames of you are still in my heart
burning alive

the flames were only placed
here when you chose the lust
painted over her moonlit body
despite the sunlight
i engraved in your universe
everyday

when you ripped out
the stitches of forever
i sewed against
the seam of your soul
that was the moment
you let me go
despite the echoes
from every valley of emptiness
of who i would be without you
desperately screaming
please
stay

LOVE WAS NEVER MEANT TO BURN THIS WAY

i thank you for the way you broke
my heart entirely into pieces
taking some of them with you
so i will never be whole again
so i will always have missing parts of me
i thank you for using me as a hotel
your pit stop on your way home leaving me
here to find my way

normally it would be back to you
but this time it is as far away
as i can get
from you
and the universe of us
we once knew

61 KM STILL TO GO

believe me
i wanted nothing more
than to walk through the gates of heaven
side by side with you
but something tells me
we were never heaven bound

it was hell loving you
it was explosive
it was hands held together begging for mercy
for these scars
these bruises
these gunshot wounds
that cover me
all of them
all of them
have your name on them

I NEVER CAME HERE LOOKING
FOR WAR
I CAME HERE LOOKING FOR
SHELTER

you say everything i touch turns to ash
that i burn all the hearts i try to love
you tell me that nothing truthful
ever came from my words
no good ever came from me being around
you ask me why i even bothered coming
back
i said to you how my whole life
you have tried to rip me apart
yet this time i have every piece of me
you threw away
swirling inside the winds in my heart
like the disaster you claimed me as
the hurricane
the storm

here i am
heading your way

IN A STATE OF AN EMERGENCY

you wash the blood off your hands
thinking the evidence has gone
down the drain
little do you know
i am the ocean you just emptied yourself into
your secret is not safe with me

for it is time
you learned how to suffer
choke
breathe under these waters

like the way you left me

TIDES OF VENGEANCE

may the truth spill so heavily out of you
that you drown in the lies
your lips have told all these years
may your tongue burn every time
you go to speak my name
for i do not belong
in the filth of your mouth

i refuse to lay
alongside the victims of your love
you have buried in the dirt of your heart
trapped in your shadows
covered in fear
just to suffocate
underneath the soil of
your love
in my own
heartache filled tears

THIS IS NOT MY FUNERAL

what did you think this was
that i was
a safe place to bury your secrets
to spill out all of your fears
what did you expect
that i would
just swallow your lies nimbly
what you should have been fearing
all along was rejection day
the day i vomit out nothing but the truth
project outward all your demons
that have been hiding in me
for they have been waiting
to come back home to you

i only kept them
to give you a chance
to run
to hide
now they are loose
here they come
and oh my dear
have they ever missed you

WELCOME HOME

as you walk around
with your scorched heart
may the stories of your scars
always remind you that
you were a fool to think you could
touch her heart of fire
without your hands burning to ash

may your lungs choke
heavily on those ashes of her
just so your tongue
will forever remember
the way her love tasted
now that she is gone
now that she belongs to your past

SWALLOWING REGRET

love became grief
the flames became a wildfire
tomorrow became a burden
the sun became a reminder
that all of the light
living inside of me
was because you put it there

ever since you left
i haven't stopped burning

I STILL FEEL YOU DEEP
IN THESE SCARS YOU LEFT ME

how dare you spill
your letters of love to me across the paper
just to crumple the page
so here now come take
a spoonful of forgiveness
from my heart for

i forgive you
i forgive you
now it is time
to forget you

GOODBYE USED TO MEAN
SEE YOU LATER NOW IT MEANS
I WISH TO NEVER SEE YOU AGAIN

to call it love
would be cruel
the way he violently
played the strings of my heart
plucking away at my fragility
deteriorating me entirely with
every stroke
i danced to his melody

while he sang
sovereignty
sovereignty

A WORLD WITHOUT THE SUN
LIFE WITHOUT THE MOON

i lay in this field
the battlefield of my heart
screaming mercy
i do not want to be a prisoner of
your love anymore
i need refuge
please stop this war
save me
write peace across my lips
breathe love into my wounds
for you are the wreckage
you started this war inside me
do not leave me here to suffer
in these walls you have me trapped in
i want to be freed
from this captivity you have caged me in
the shade of oppression
has coloured my lips for far too long
so here is my white flag
i am throwing up my hands
what more could you possibly want
you have my heart

i surrender
i surrender

BATTLE CRY

tongue tied in knots
the alexithymia has the best of me
searching for my existence
before you embedded the rest of me
if only life had a delete button
to rid yourself
of the mistakes that you make

i would erase everything
to have myself back
even if the means were forgetting you

DETOX

i held on for so long
even when the rope of your love
started disintegrating in my hands
when my heart began deteriorating
when your love started feeling like knives
and your words left nothing
but these holes burning through me

you set me on fire
just to watch me go up in flames
you loved that you had the power
the choice to
burn me
love me
or leave me

**HERE ARE MY LIFELINES ALL
ATTACHED TO YOU**

walking away from me
could you not see
the sky falling
a fire in the forest starting
the ocean rising
all in unison with my heart
cracking burning drowning
all this love you gave me
burning out
collapsing

how oh how
could you not see
you were the core centrepiece of me

CALL IT A SUPERNOVA EXPLOSION

no matter how much
i wished
i prayed
i begged
love was always
the fault in my heart
the burnout amid my stars
for no matter how bad
i wanted us to happen

i was never yours
you were never mine
a love like ours
was never meant to be

BATTLING THE HANDS OF FATE
ONLY ONE WALKS AWAY THE
WINNER

our love has become so crowded
i can barely fit
in between these walls around us
there is no room
since we have become
the space
the darkness
the emptiness
when did we move
into this house of resentment
this is no home
without us
without you
i cannot stay here any longer
my invitation into your heart
has come and gone
our love here is expired
we are long
overdue

BLACKOUT CURTAINS

the hardest part
of having loved you
and having lost you
is forever
having to exist within this corpse

the space you forgot
to love me back

BURDENS OF HEARTBREAK

they say it gets easier
that time heals everything
the pain will go away
they say the heart will mend
you will be able to move on
that what you feel is temporary however
when it comes to losing someone
how can you fill the void
the space where they used to be
how can you say time will heal you
how can it
for that hole where they used to be
will always be a huge gap
and you will only destroy yourself
replaying memories and moments of them
that only make you miss them more
that feeling of missing someone
it is not temporary
it will not pass
time will never be able to bring them back
or make you miss them less
the clock ticks
to the sound of your heart breaking
a little more each and every
passing day

FUNERALS

watching you leave
was not nearly as hard
as coming back home
just to find pieces of you
and the remains of your love

still here
all over me

ABANDONED SHIPS

i often beg the moon
to show me the sky
of what our world
once looked like before
i love you
started to sound like a lie

we sat underneath a warfare sky
our lungs filled with smoke
from the remains of our universe
burning
and all the stars we once
wished upon
were exploding
we both knew the hourglass of our love
had run out of time

my memory took me back to
that night late in september
when you really left
how i sat inside the walls of our love
staring at the door
thinking any second you would come back
that was the moment i realized how much
i loved you
as my soul left my body and departed
with you
my heart bled for hours
days
weeks
i sat wiping my eyes with loneliness
sleeping beside dreams of nostalgia
you walked away from me
confidently free
while i knew i would always feel you
deep in these scars you left me

looking at you for the last time
all my heart could feel was pain
the pain of counting every dead forever
you once said
the pain of knowing i still love you
i do not know how to stop loving you
i will always love you
even though the fire of our love has died out

forever can mean heaven
forever can mean hell
i know where you are
can you take a guess
where i am

SUMMER ON THE CRISP OF AUTUMN

when the night comes
crawling
i cannot help but wonder
if you feel lonely too
without me
without us
without love
like i am
without you

missing you is an understatement

my body has yet found shelter
since you once walked my lands
and imprinted the word
exile
on my bones
when you left

1000 DAYS WITHOUT YOU

the only thing i ever needed from you was
for you to tell me you need me just as much too

ARRIVAL

i remember it
the sun was hiding that day
tucked away behind a shield of clouds
the air was frightening
bone chilling
as if the most brutal winter storm
was about to touch down
in the pit of my soul
it was as if my world was trying to tell me
every beginning has an end
and this was it
the end
collapsing beneath me

every morning the roses in the garden
would softly smile back at me
that day they never did thorns
all i felt was thorns
piercing my flesh deeply

like the earth losing colour on
the cusp of winter
the sky preparing for the arrival of dusk
saying goodbye to the passing dawn
the tree's gathering to swallow their
last breath of summer
before they shed their skin

we need to die
we need to let go
to grow
to be reborn

i thought the sun would never rise again
the day your love left me
the day you left me
until today
watching you fade into the tail of darkness
as the sun set
i saw nothing but a million suns rising
aching to pour the light back into
every scar your love left me
i did not realize letting you go
shedding the skin of your love
would reveal the roots of my flesh
still here
holding me

the departure
the dusk of you
became the arrival
the dawn of me

A LIFETIME OF SUNSHINE

when you split open
the seams of grief
your wounds will find

a whole world of growth

i was born into this world hungry
like the way my mother's bones
desperately ached for love

i was born into this world thirsty
like the fiend imprisoned in my father
whose desire to feed his demons
meant more than his own daughters love

you cursed me with those same addictions
you buried them ten feet under my skin
you left me to live in a house
burning with abandonment
only to torture myself with the absence
of all the things we could have been

the only question
that still breaks my ribcage apart
every time my tongue
goes to swallow your name is

did you ever think one day
i would take all the fire you left here
only to burn me
and light the wick of redemption within?

GROWING PAINS

when you offered them *refuge*
they turned you into a **ruin**
when you built them a *home*
inside of your heart
they made an **asylum** out of you
can't you hear the moon cry
every time you say
your bones were only made for
breaking

how there are rooms inside of your body
where abandonment lives now
empty hallways dripping with
shades of loneliness
how the walls of your memory still
tell stories of how you were once
screaming colour
so alive
how your skin is still begging
for you to come back home
how the light switches in your veins
are dying to be reborn
from the darkness again
just to watch the way your soul
used to dance
softly underneath the moonlight

all of this destruction they caused
leaves more room for rebuilding
so break open those aching bones
build back the garden of kindness
that they wilted in your soul
dust off the cobwebs
rip open the curtains of your heart
so you can feel the light
burning
pouring life back into your skin
burning

you were born with
fire
water
earth
air
in your soul
no matter how many times
you need to rebirth
you were built to survive

YOU WILL SURVIVE THIS

has anyone ever told you
how gracious survival looks on you
the way your hands have carried
centuries of war
yet you still touch the hearts of others
kindly
softly
with oceans of love

has anyone ever told you
how phenomenal survival looks on you
the way your body has become
a battlefield
from every time they came with knives
to carve out all the parts of you
yet you still find the strength
to grab your broken bones
to stitch up the liberty
they tried to rip out of your soul

has anyone ever told you
how stunning survival looks on you
you are painted in tribulation
your body is coloured
with sorrow filled bruises
you smell like you have spent
years running with the wolves
yet you never hide
when the sun comes crawling
out of the sky
wanting to expose your scars
instead you sing survival with her

this is the way the gods built you
war will come
to break apart your bones
to tear your flesh apart
but what is there to fear
when you have a warrior spirit
running wild
screaming survival
inside

THE DAWN OF HALLEY'S COMET

if i could rip open
the edges of your soul
i would carry the sun from the sky
to bathe your brokenness
in waters of gold
i would summon the river to flow
inside the chambers of your heart
pumping life back into your veins
flushing out the decaying parts of
your broken body
of your wilted bones
i would light the wick inside
all of the haunted places in you
while silently watching
the fire burn down
the house you made for yourself
out of darkness
gently reminding you how

you are an overflowing ocean
before
they ever came to tell you
you were just a deserted shore

JOSEPHINE

you have been quietly carrying around
the remains of what abandonment left you
it was only a matter of time
until you became a walking graveyard
time never taught you
how to let go of what leaves you
fear only taught you
how to carry
how to suffocate
how to bury yourself
under the soil of grief
while you watch the world take everything
you have ever loved
all of this emptiness has turned you
into a ruin
you forgot how every night you die
with the ghost of who you were yesterday
and every morning you wake
with the sunlight dripping into your soul

time never told you
how beautiful grief is
grief is what makes us grow
the dusk calls for our passing
but the dawn
oh the dawn
that is when we are reborn

THE WAR WITHIN OUR BONES

listen to your angels
when they tell you
how much beauty is buried beneath
your brokenness
when the gods sculpted you
they made your heart out of clay
so you would
break
crumble
fall apart
to learn the art
of rebuilding yourself

THERAPY SESSIONS

recovery

that is what i will call this
scraped knees
bleeding heart
bruised lungs

all together still
crawling
beating
breathing

damaged
not doomed
for a crack never meant broken
simply more room for the flowers
to come through
and bloom

APRIL THUNDERSHOWERS

slowly
the words begin to need the paper
the darkness starts to beg to feel
the light
the sun cannot fall asleep
if the moon gives up on loving her
at night
we bleed
we cry
we suffer
immensely
until our hearts have no choice
to forgive the pain
or to become the pain

I HOPE YOU ALWAYS CHOOSE
THE FIRST ONE

if there is one thing to know
about an artist

be careful with what
kind of *fuel*
you throw into their *fire*

someone out there just lost their mother
grief just became the heaviness
they will carry on their back
for the next century
they have to live without her
this is when they need that hug
they need that reminder
that they still have your love
to hold onto

someone out there was just diagnosed
with cancer
a deadline for how many suns
they get to awaken to
how many moons left
until they permanently fall asleep
this is when they need you the most
to remind them they are a warrior
and in this kind of war
they will walk out on the
other side screaming
victory
defeat

someone out there just lost their job
fear just became the poison
flooding their veins
survival begins to look a lot like
their starving daughter
life begins to feel like a fight
this is when they need you to tell them
they will get through this
a storm does not last forever
the sun will rise again

someone out there is battling depression
any second they are ready to give up
to pull the plug
they do not want to feel this heaviness
anymore
this is when they need you to tell them
you will carry them
when their nights go moonless
and they cannot remember
how to carry themselves
you will grab the sun and shine
a world of healing
inside the dark parts of their soul
you will teach them again
how to breathe

with every person you meet
touch them with hands of kindness
bathe them in oceans of gentleness
show compassion with your words
help them fight the wars they are
battling inside

HOW TO BE HUMAN

for every night you spent
ripping yourself apart
underneath the moon
i promise every morning you wake
for the rest of your lifetime
i will carry the sunrise
across the ocean
to you

I WANT TO BATHE
YOUR SOUL IN GOLD

your heart
is a mountain
built of diamonds
your soul
is an empire
made of gold

if they cannot see this
exists inside of you

please gently
let them go

SELF WORTH

sew your words
with threads of forgiveness
so you never have to wilt
waiting for apologies
from those who have hurt you
they were never taught
the power of

i am sorry

they are too busy believing
it is those words
that make them weak

ATONEMENT

maybe goodbye is a word
you need to teach your tongue
to grasp better
so that your hands will learn
to stop reopening
the doors of the past
once they have closed
so that your heart will stop
believing the tales of lust
fooling you to pour
all of you
all of your love
into people who were never taught
how to stay long enough
to make love last
who will never fully see you
your heart
your soul
as a whole
they will only see you as an achromatic
half empty glass

SHADES OF INDIFFERENCE

they told you
to wipe the depression off your face
as if you can pick up a paintbrush
and paint over the places under your skin
that are drenched in darkness

they told you
to take off the layer of grief your heart wears
as if it is a sweater that is out of season
a size too small for the heaviness
you carry around on your back

they told you
to throw away the words
anorexia
suicide
anxiety
asking you

how can something so beautiful
be poisoned with so much pain?

.

as if you are diseased
as if you are something that needs to be fixed
they cannot see their words
their hands
their hearts
have the ability to do this

(to break you like this)

please tell me your soul never soaked up
the filth of their words
please tell me your mind never birthed
a place for this darkness to exist
in your world

(this darkness is theirs not yours)

these kinds of people will never understand
the beauty of breaking
they are too busy convincing people
they are the cure
yet it is these people
who break the hardest
who cry the loudest

when **they told you** all of these things
it is because they
hurt the same way
hurt by someone else

a stranger
their wife
husband
mother
father

they were fed this poison
from words
that were built
on centuries of negativity

so be the person who shows them kindness
be the person who in return
takes the sun from the sky
and showers them with positivity
this is what we all need
so we can learn

HOW TO HEAL FROM THE INSIDE OUT

i have yet to see
another sunrise
spill across the sky
and awaken me

like you do

in the end we are all
oceans running wild
bleeding rivers of chaos
wildfires burning with passion
soldiers fighting the turmoil
the world built into our bones

in the end love will always win
it is the most powerful energy
the most beautiful drug
it has the ability to save us
heal us
to turn any darkness flooding through
our veins into gold

in the end we are all addicts
because an addict is not just
an alcoholic or a drug user
it is the child who spends centuries
looking for the love
their parents never gave them
it is the artist who needs the pen
to silence their demons
to paint their pain away
it is the man of society who believes
money is worth more than the time
on the clock passing by him everyday

in the end we are all just
high off a certain kind of love
addicted to a certain kind of madness
built of the same anatomy
stitched together by the hands of the universe

we all bleed humility
we all bleed humanity

SILENT CRIES OF SOCIETY

[credits to the beautiful soul @nikkirootbeer]

someone will come along
and touch you in places
where you never thought it was possible
to ever feel the light there again
someone will come along
and start a wildfire inside your heart
you will be aflame with desire
they will give you a kind of love
you will forever feel igniting light
through the skyline of your soul
someone will come along
and you will softly swallow the word

stay

so the vacancy left in your veins
from years of loving the wrong ones
can finally

leave

someone will come along
and teach you a whole language of love
where midnight and loneliness
are never used in the same sentence
they will spell your name with stars
and you will spend the rest of your life
knowing what it means to be
good enough
wanted enough
needed enough
loved enough

you will feel love
burning
for an eternity
throughout the universe beneath your skin
straight into the depths of your soul

NEVADA SUNRISE

open the windows of your heart and listen closely
to the sound of the stars singing survival for you at night

love should feel like
the breath of all your troubles
softly exhaling

finally
finally
i am home

SHELTER

do not choose the ones who cannot say
i love you
without looking away
do not choose the ones who have you
wilting
sitting by the phone
as if love is a waiting game

they were never planning to come anyway

do not choose the ones you know
you would swim across an ocean for
and they cannot even give you
ten minutes of their day
do not choose the ones who make you feel
like loving you is grim

you will regret the day you abandon your
softness for them

instead

choose the ones who pour the light
back into your soul
on the days you do not know
how to carry yourself
on the days you feel like
the sun will never rise

chase the ones who are not afraid
to build a world around you
who celebrate your existence
in every way
who ignite fires of love inside the darkest
places of your soul everyday

choose the ones that inspire you
to become a better person
chase the ones that do not tell you
they love you
they show you
they love you
then they gently teach you
how to love
how to also choose
yourself

EDEN

let me in
beside the aching loneliness
beside all of the places
the world told you to hide
let me love you
all of those parts of you
until you are ready
to crawl back into your skin
until you feel safe inside

SOLITUDE

if we are what we attract
then carry an infinite ocean of love
inside of your heart and

spill it everywhere you go

it is within these
scars
your love left me

that i will learn
how to love
myself

SURVIVING YOU

dear heart of mine

i apologize for continuously wearing you
on my sleeve
so the hands of lust
are able to touch you
for blaming these wars
of pandemonium
on your tender seams
when you have been the only one
to stitch the pieces i have lost
back together
for being the only organ in my body
who fights for the weaker side of me
the one who tells my hands
to pick me up off the bathroom floor
when nothing but tragedy and ache
spill out from my soul at night
for showing me these threads
these stitches
you have sewn in me
are reminders
despite those who have stayed
despite those who have left

i am still deserving of love
i am love

REVELATIONS

without scars
we would not know strength
we would not know resilience
we would not know bravery
the scars that paint our bodies
show the depths we have loved
the wars we have fought
the battles we have won
the addictions we have overcome
the storms we have endured
everything we have survived
these scars remind us
even though we bleed
we cry
we hurt
we suffer
over and over again
the creator within us
will always prosper
the survivor inside us
will always get back up
our wounds will always heal
because we are warriors
and through the depths of our scars
we will always rise

NEVER BE ASHAMED OF YOUR BATTLE SCARS

every time i kiss you
all i can taste is your pain
i watch you dress every morning
covering up your shame cutting
open your heart
just to drain
all the memories haunting you
intoxicating your veins
you believe that love
is something that you do not
deserve to receive
yet come here my love
look a little bit closer
what you fail to see
is the ocean of art you bleed

you embody the meaning of a
breathing
hurting
beautiful
ethereal masterpiece

AN UNFORGETTABLE MUSE

in the final hours of the day
when the sky turns into night
and the cracks in your heart
are begging to feel any kind of light
i will ask the heavens to let me borrow
the sky
to show you the galaxy
you carry underneath your skin
how oh how
you are everything tied into one

the moon
the stars
the sun

you are nothing but divine light

FIREFLIES

there is something
so dangerous
yet so liberating
talking to a stranger
the way they look at you
for who you are in that exact moment

standing
breathing
deservingly existing
in space
in time
no holding you against tomorrow
nor looking at you
amongst the shadows of your past

JANUARY 1st

you made a garden of roses grow inside
her heart where they said nothing beautiful
could ever come from such
distressed grounds
when they said love could never be found
in the potholes
in the cracks of her soul
you laughed saying carpenters were made
to fix things
to rebuild what has been destroyed
better than before
when they said it would cost a fortune to repair
the parts of her that are missing
that have broken down
you smiled saying how a good mechanic
does the job purely out of love
out of passion
not for cost
not for money
when they looked at you astounded asking
what is it that makes you
love her like this
you simply said
every piece of art is a masterpiece
every painting is worth something
to someone and to me
 she is worth the whole damn world

THE ART OF KINTSUKUROI

there is a difference
between coming home
and coming home
to you

SUNDAY MORNINGS

i want to be the one whose fingerprints
embed forever
on the outline of your body
i want to be the one who colours
all your thoughts filling all the spaces
between your heart and mind
i want to be the one
who plants the sempiternal seeds
within the pit of your soul
so our love will never run out of time
so together we will always grow

ELYSIAN VISIONS

love was beyond
ephemeral physicality to me

it was finding you
with all of the lights off amongst
the darkness of my heart
and having your love be
the only light
i could see

LUMINOUS COLLISIONS

our bodies were never boundaries
or restricting limits

i fell in love with your soul
long before i fell in love
with the landscape of your skin

PLACES TO CALL HOME

it was 9:36 p.m.
the exact moment i looked at you
with the feel of wanderlust awakening
the lust in my veins

it was that moment
the alexithymia silenced all my words
and my body convinced my mind to
stay

BAD HABITS

poetry whispered

spill yourself all over these walls
paint them with the motions of your
body
colour them with the secrets of your
soul
expose all that is hidden beneath your
skin
the art i crave
lies in the mess you leave behind

EXPLOSIONS OF LOVE

baby
they touched your body
not your soul

you deserve to be loved
to be felt
deeper than the surface
of your skin
you deserve to be loved
so much more

RUINS OF LUST

one day you will wake up and
taste her in your coffee
or you will feel him on your fingertips
like you just touched him
they can be a thousand miles away
buried seven years in the past
yet if love ever sparked from your heart
you will always remember
the person who started the fire

she will always burn in your heart
and the fireworks will
always and forever
spell his name

THE UNFORGETTABLE ONES

the light of your soul ignites a wildfire inside my bones
you will forever be my awakening

you are used to the sold sign going up
on the hearts of people
you have made a home out of
forced to pack up your memories
and leave everything behind
so you move to a new city
where this time
you are going to build a home inside
yourself
without him
without her
for you are tired
of people always leaving
of always being lost

it is time the lights turn on
inside a heart that has spent
far too much time hiding in the dark

SAFE HAVEN

i know these moments will pass
i will meet up with myself in time
five minutes from now
three months from now
seven years from now
in this moment i may be lost
but i know i am hiding
somewhere out there
perhaps in a city i have not yet traveled
        to
or in the heart of a stranger
i have not yet loved

WANDERLUST

he did not name her after a comet
to let darkness overshadow her light
he did not sell her to the heavens
to become a falling star at night
she was a seventh wonder to this world
made entirely of angel dust
and blood pumping strands
of lethal wanderlust

YOUNG GOD

she had a temper like lightning
a heart deep like the ocean
eyes full of celestial love
lungs filled with shooting stars
just as much as she was sweet
like honey
she was just as deadly
as a tropical storm
she was a balance
between everything dark
and all things light
while some would say
she reminded them of shades
within the sunrise
others would say
phases of the moon

VAGARY SILHOUETTES

you are nothing but a ray of sunshine
with stardust colouring
the light in your eyes
as you pass by there is nothing
but trails of grace that you leave behind
and the way you leak love
all over this world
has me believing
you are the means
to heaven on earth

ANGELS WHO WALK AMONG US

there will be days you will
feel like the moon
one half of you buried in the
loneliness
woven into the craters covering
your skin
the other half aching to shed
your heaviness
so you can finally dive
into the waters of
desire

then there will be days you will
feel like the sun
some parts of you wanting to
remain hidden in the fires of love
while the other parts of you
want to burst into flames
just to feel the euphoria
of burning wildly
alive

DIVIDED EQUALLY

always remember who you were
before this all
before him
before her
never forget that you
exist in a world that will try
to sedate you
intoxicate you
corrupt every part of you
remember death is inevitable
the goal is to figure out
what it means to be
alive

THE ACT OF SURVIVAL

black was her hair
her eyes
her exterior
before he cut
her open to show
her she bleeds red
bleeds life
bleeds love

she is painted
rich in colour within
it just took someone
to reveal
the galaxy
the masterpiece she was
hidden underneath her skin

THE STATE OF DENUDATION

with the stars in the sky build a pathway
a road that will always lead me to you
start a fire when i am lost in the darkness
burn me with light
so i can see you
there is not a day that will pass
i will not miss you
so spill yourself in everything i do
be the wind in my hair when i am walking
haunt me just so i can feel you

STARING THROUGH THE GATES OF HEAVEN

may the moonlight comfort you
through the darkness of your night
may the sunrise carry you
with all of its light
the stars hold you together
with all the heavens' might
to remind your weary heart
you were born with purpose
and to survive
means to fight

MACLEOD

if the chambers of lucifer
keep you in captivity
so you can never fully wake
to feel the sun
remember that you are heaven bound
despite what those demons whisper
underneath your skin
and though you may have fallen
the wings on your back
are a testimony of redemption
for the gods hold the gates open
waiting covetously for your return

RED CARPETS

in the same moment
we are holding on
we are also letting go
of our silhouette hearts
of our compulsive self-control
for in our darkest hour
it consumes us whole

may we throw up our flags
and surrender to the unknown

FROM THE ASHES

our flaw rests within our hunger
our desire to obtain one another
through the body
losing
appreciation
to know
to see
to understand one another
through our roots
beneath the soil of our soul

WEEDS OF LUST

they ask me why i never want to stay
why i always show up
with the intent to walk away
why i hide my heart beside the exit sign
why i am only visible
when you look between the lines

what they do not know
is my feet only know how to run
that i have spent my whole life searching
for heaven
through all the hell
i come from

METAMORPHOSIS

look beyond the worn-out stitches
holding together every crack in your soul
underneath all the scars
that colour your body beautiful
for that is the place you will
find yourself
find real beauty
in between the lines of
all of your madness
all of your chaos
all of your pain

FINDING A LATIBULE

i always saw her rain clouds
as the heavens' way
of watering her soul
for only in time
was she bound to grow
out from the cracks in the concrete
into a rose

RESILIENCE

the ones who truly love you
will never leave you
the ones who truly love you
no matter what will stay

these are the words we chant to the stars
yet these are the words that still
rip apart our hearts
why do we give so much to hands
who were only taught how to take
why do we break our backs
building homes for people
who never plan to stay
this torturous cycle ends when we start
protecting the oceans of love we carry
within ourselves
for even they have endings too
stop pouring
stop draining
stop emptying
out yourself for others
instead
start protecting
start filling
start pouring all of this love back
inside yourself
you need it more than they ever will

REVIVAL

god gave her fingertips
to turn her world into poetry
filled her with crystal lights
to see things in perfect symmetry
a transparency to exist behind
the subconscious memory
and a type of love to spill out
of you for a thousand
centuries

MOUTH FULL OF POETRY

some would call
her a mess
a disaster
a storm passing by
some would say
she is just a dreamer
a little girl
a lost soul
then there were those
who felt her presence
saw her heart
her halo
her light
and knew she was just
like the rest of us trying to survive

she just had her own way of doing it

THE LIFE OF A BUTTERFLY

you have spent so much time running
trying to find home
that you have forgotten about
the four walls that you come
home to every night

now that my darling
is a place that will only abandon you
the nights you abandon yourself

THE HOUSE UNDER YOUR SKIN

do you ever wonder
if the universe has been here hiding
inside of you
this whole entire time
the doors are wide open
they have been for years
it was your mind who convinced
your hands
the doors were locked

ALCHEMY

all we have is our rhymes
our poetic minds
writing truth from
the roots of our soul
til our pens bleed dry
in all the ways we
stir up these riots inside
to paint the world with our art
spreading hope
spreading fire
so one day
we can look death in the eye
without fear
for through our stories
we are legends
we will never die

IMMORTALITY IS THE INK
FEEDING AN ARTISTS PEN

i will learn to swim
through the storms of my life
picking up all the pieces of myself
that get lost along the way
letting the moonlight fill these holes
love has only burned through me
shoving the word disaster
back down the mouths of strangers
who claim i am only a wreckage

for i am not lost only
seeking refuge
for out there must exist a place
my heart can finally
touch solid ground
just to know the feeling
of being loved
of being found

HOWLING WOLVES

they talk about you
as if they know you
you become tied up
in their filthy mouths
vomiting your name
all over each other's thoughts
setting fire to your name
they want to see you
burn up in smoke
to fall as ash on the floor
only to then blow away
they talk about you like
you are disposable
trying to find that crack
to break you
thinking you have
a glass heart to shatter
fragile bones

yet what they do not know is
you have angels in your hair
the moon on your side
let them play those games
while you sail opposite tides

THE POWER IN THE UNSEEN

do not let your past
fool your future
into believing
that time is the enemy
do not let yourself fade beyond
recognition
do not let them convince you that
being drenched in faith
within the midst of a storm
means that you are drowning
for faith will be
the anchor that saves you
until you have made peace
with your demons
and all the darkness you
have been running from
within the ridge of your soul
becomes the light
to lead you back home

UNDER CONSTRUCTION

it will always be a fight
it will always be a battle
conquering darkness with light
paralyzing pain with love
threading wings
onto your demons of the night
swallowing addictions
hoping on the other side
you are still there
somewhere in sight
for those indomitable torches
in your mind
give you that choice
to be the fire
or to fear the fire

there is no other way out

PROTAGONIST VERSUS ANTAGONIST

*when the flesh of my body decays to the core of my bones
i will miss the way the sunlight danced
across your shoulders every july*

they say she is an angel
cursed with a weeping cry
a blessing in disguise
that her middle name is survival
for even in the midst of a storm
her fists rise with fire
ready for battle
ready to thrive
no matter the depths of the ash
the phoenix within her
will always rise

the burns from the fires
the scars covering her body
all healed with her triumph
proving she was far from weak
her veins are filled with light
so strong
not even the darkest storm
can conquer her heart
or bring defeat

WHAT IS THERE TO FEAR
WHEN YOU ARE THE FIRE?

we only have two options love

grow together
or grow apart

THE STATE OF KENOPSIA

lay down with me
show me all of your scars
bring me to the chambers
fear has you trapped in
let me see your bleeding heart

i will tell you now regardless
nothing will stop my love
from wanting to know
the parts of you hidden each
night the lights go down

i crave to touch
to know
to love
all of your darkness

DANCING IN THE MOONLIGHT

let me defrost the winter in your lungs
so you can finally feel summer again
for you deserve to feel something
after a century of being numb
so inhale my love
until it becomes your oxygen
until it kills the pain
and becomes your favourite drug

PRESCRIPTIONS

i am not denying
the fact we define chemistry
or trying to alter the path of destiny
yet essentially when you are next to me
it is ecstasy
for chemically
you spread through my veins
causing melodies and symphonies
that endlessly replay

THE TASTE OF IMPRESSIONS

time has promised us
this moment is ours only
to discover the galaxies
hidden underneath our skin
to find raw beauty
uncut and uncensored
to rely on our senses
to navigate these maps
painted on our bodies

we are explorers
and tonight may
we find our way home

EXPEDITIONS

i loved him for the way
he kissed my demons goodnight
i loved him even more
for the way he would wake
in the morning
and the phosphene in his eyes
would fall upon me
as if heaven was something
illuminating his sight

KALOPSIAN DREAMS

with lungs filled from the fumes of you
i lay here breathlessly
while fireworks explode inside my chest
my heart beats heavily
ironically the feel of you is heavenly
causing episodic memory
to revive me mentally
for love has not tasted
this good
in over a century

SOLE FOCUS

i tossed love into the strings
of your heart
hoping to hear a symphony reciprocated
to have the beat of my heart
synchronize with yours
become replicated
to have the vibrations in between
each breath illustrated
uniting as strands of violet
in the love
we just created

CHROMESTHESIA

in the end
it did not matter
my heart leaked holy water
every shade of sin
still coloured my lips

it was the angel in me
who found love
in the devil in him

HANDS ON THE BIBLE

i imagined it would be explosive
when our souls came into contact
for the sun just told me
she is jealous of the way we burn bright
and the heavens are begging to feel our
        light
while all the planets
crave to exist in this universe
we call our love
at night

PART II

not even the sun or the moon
could illuminate my body
the way that you do
even though
i belong to the stars
heaven is where i live
my heart
still comes back home
every night to you

EXTRATERRESTRIAL PAINTINGS

i want you to find me
through the threads of these sheets
through my wine-stained lips dripping
through the desperation in my heartbeat
i want you to search
until your hands find their way home
on the curves of my body
in the depths of my soul

VIBRATIONS

you ask me how
i want you

in trails of whispers that fill my heart
with secrets unknown
in moonlit sidewalks that bring me home
each night to you
in a way where i am stripped
naked of my fears
and your love is the shield that
armours me
clothes me

love me in such a way
that even the stars above
would be jealous
of the galaxy of words
you have painted across
the sky for me

THROWING WISHES INTO
SHOOTING STARS

all i ever want
all i ever wanted
was you
even if that meant your demons
came along with you too
for nothing in my life
ever made sense
until you were in my view
i knew my love
even if it turned to pain would
never look as good
on anyone else
as it would on you

TUNNEL VISION

we went deep-sea diving
and found love anchored
to the bottom of the ocean floor
so we carved our initials in the stones
for it was the wanderlust
running through those waters
that convinced me
you felt just like home
even if the currents persuade us
otherwise
it will be these anchors
that are the reason
i could never let you go

i know the depth of this love despite
where on land we roam

SWIMMING AGAINST THE ODDS

i cannot control the appetency
my mind has fallen victim
to you
my desire to taste more than
your body
your thoughts
i cannot tame or restrict
the side of me that wants
nothing more than to devour
to consume
to be filled with
every inch
every piece of you

INCIPIENT HEARTBEATS

without them
nothing makes sense
without them
you remain black and white blurred
between the lines

with them
you are invincible
with them
your world bleeds nothing but colour
with them
you feel nothing but alive

OXYGEN

i could tell you in a thousand ways
why i love you
but even then it still
would not be enough
how can you repay someone
who saw a light in you
that you did not know existed
who devours even the most
bitter taste of your words
who makes love to your whole body
when all along you thought you were
just broken bones
bound to this bruised soul

ART GALLERIES

when people leave you
when love leaves you
when relationships leave you
when your job leaves you
when friends leave you
all in your darkest hour
finding the light can seem impossible
i promise you it is not
go for a walk with your solitude
cook your favourite meal
listen to your favourite song on repeat 10 times
get lost in the world of your favourite book
sit at your favourite cafe
order a drink
observe how beautiful the life around you is
let it sink into the ocean of your soul
how we are all here on this planet
sharing this borrowed time
trying to create life from our flesh and bones
when something leaves you
i promise you a better purpose will find you
if not today
then tomorrow
something will come and touch
every part of you drowning in darkness
it could be love
a stranger
a new passion
even yourself
the light is everywhere
waiting to find you
go find it

HEALING REMEDIES

he felt like the moment
you stop running
when your feet know
you have arrived home
the love i had for him was enough
to rot my bones
consume me whole
yet i never hesitated
for i have never
wanted to drown myself
more beautifully in the waters of love

i have never wanted anything more

WHEN THE RIPPLE MEETS
THE TIDE

p.s.

i see you entirely
hands covered in burns
from always trying to catch
the flames of love
for all your old lovers
have only burned fuses
throughout your body
leaving you with scars
deep enough you can still feel
your past

yet tonight in my presence
you have nothing to fear
i intend to set your heart on fire
with a love to ignite you
with a love that will never
turn your heart into ash

PHOENIX

lay down
right here
next to me
bodies asleep
through the soul
i want to meet
to touch you with the
thrill of desire
the way you deserve

ethereally deep

WHEN THE ARTIST MEETS THE MUSE

the pen of my heart will continue
to bleed
colours of you
colours of me
we were just a blank page
until the chaos claimed
our love and turned our scars
into a masterpiece

BEAUTIFUL DISASTERS

he never feared my fire
he never feared my storm
he begged to make love to the wolf
trapped underneath my bones
just to taste the freedom
running through
the wilderness of my soul

WILD HEARTS

every moment with him
was pure ecstasy
he was my remedy
for his love
was the only drug
strong cnough to calm
every hurricane
every storm happening inside of me

THE FADE OUT AFTER A
KALEIDOSCOPIC DREAM

if only we could capture this moment
preserve this feeling
we could have love forever
without expiration
for despite what they say
i do not need translation
for you cannot explain
a whole language of love
to people who only read abbreviations

TWENTY-SIX LETTERS

you have become the ink
that bleeds from the tips of my fingers
embedded within the memories
held by my palms
for my hands will always long
to touch you
to know you
to reach for you
to write of you

I AM ADDICTED TO
DISCOVERING
GALAXIES OF YOU

when my heart went to war for you
i knew it would be a losing battle
against all my logic
against all my sanity
for the taste of you
remained in my memories
the feel of you in my veins
and despite part of me
wanting you permanently
gone
there was still a part of me
who desperately
needed you to
stay

CARAPHERNELIA

no amount of time
or nepenthean
could erase you from
the depths of my subconscious
i did not just love you with
my open eyes
i dreamt of worlds of you
before we met
all that remains
are nostalgic feelings impossible
to forget

HALCYON DAYS

i hope you find a love
who always calls back
who never shows up late
who pulls you closer than
you have ever been held
through the middle of the night
who never again makes you question
the word *stay*

who touches you so wild
you believe again in the hands of fate
who does not rob you
of your softness nor grace
who instead renovates the parts of you
that you have labeled damaged
that you keep hidden away

who plants flowers in your lungs
so the smell of roses
awakens you each day
who turns all of your scars into gold
who shows you how much beauty
that your scars hold
who makes the blood in your veins
triumphantly rise
who only says i will see you later
who never has believed in the word
goodbye

i hope you find someone
who makes love
to your passions
someone who sees the fire
the universe
behind your eyes

i hope you find a love
that makes you feel
nothing but
alive
who will always always always
take the time to watch your
sunrise

COTTON CANDY SKIES

i would drown a thousand times in your waters
if love ever came to the shore and told me
once more i could be yours

SHADOWS

i keep having these midnight conversations
with my heart
trying to convince myself that
letting go of you
does not mean i am
letting go of me
but something about the way the stars
look beside the moon tonight
tells me differently

there are oceans inside my veins
that will always carry you
there are walls you built
all over my body that still have
the word
infinity
carved on them
there are stories i still tell of us
because my tongue has not figured out yet
how to forget your name
and every time it slips out from the cracks
in between my teeth
they throw the word **_addiction_** at me
like you are a bad habit
a cigarette i need to stop smoking
a bottle of whiskey i do not need
as if there is a way i can rid myself of you
like you are some lethal disease

when they told me
my only true antidote
was to find the strength to let you go
i knew they could not help with what
they cannot see

how do you beg your body
to stop surviving off the blood your
heart bleeds
how can i quit you
when you are that same blood running
through my veins
that my body needs
that i need

I COULD NOT QUIT YOU
EVEN IF I WANTED TO

i knew i would lose myself
i knew you would win
i knew the war
you would cause inside me
by letting you in
yet i would have rather
loved you and lost you
than to never have
let these wars of love begin

PAPER THIN

his love was the type
you can feel trapped inside
your pulmonary veins
the type of love that drowns you
in an ocean of poetic distortion
where you cannot decipher
the mess
in your heart
the chaos
in your head
if love's intention

is to drown
or to save

IN THE HANDS OF AN ARCHITECT

your absence is felt
through every part of me
with every beat
my heart aches with anticipation

so i keep these flames
of love burning inside me
just in case you ever decide you
miss me
you miss us
you want to come back home

THE CITY I BUILT FOR YOU

before the chaos
we were stitched together
in perfect synchrony
separation never quivered upon
our lips when we spoke of
infinity
now as we unravel
the feel of your threads
is distressed affinity
for in the seam of your love
i lay patched here

distantly

SUEDE TO LEATHER

there i am
gathering all the pieces of our love
to try and sell to someone else
there i am
peeling off every piece of you
left on me
trying to wash off the scent of you
of every fallen memory
i figured if i could take
you out of me
i would be free
but here i am standing
face to face with myself
and an unfamiliar face is all i see

without you
gone is my identity
gone is me

SELF DISCOVERY

even after you left
i continued to love you
i could not fathom
the thought of erasing you
with the sound of a goodbye
so i let myself love you
amongst the silence
until every drop of love
i had for you in my heart and veins
bled completely dry

THE ART OF DESICCATION

i swam through the depths of the ocean
to try and save you
ran through the blazing fires in the forest
to try and find you
i burned my hands every time
i went to touch you
i sacrificed so much of myself
trying to love you
only to find you were already saved and
i was the one
who needed saving

911 WHAT IS YOUR EMERGENCY?

i sentenced my heart to this turmoil
the second i became the artist and
he became my muse
every canvas i paint
drips with shades of vemod
numinous spectrums
reflecting the love we once knew
to let the paintbrush dry
is a death sentence
is pulling the plug
on a life
on a love
far too soon

SHADES OF SAUDADE

the water of my heart was not enough
to fill the ocean in your eyes
the air in my lungs was not enough
to breathe our love back to life
not enough persuasion
in my words to convince
time to bring you back
a love that is never good enough
now what is the point of that

WE WERE NEVER MEANT
TO SEE THE SUNRISE

the beginning was so bright
that nobody could have predicted
the end would be this dark
i guess just like light bulbs
love burns out too
and so do the flames in our hearts
we may have the light
the love
trapped inside our eyes
but we still need to close them at night
maybe
that is where i went wrong
i never opened my eyes again
i did not want to
i feared
you would not even be there
be here

DAYDREAMS TURNED INTO NIGHTMARES

wait
come back
before you exit my heart
take everything you built
inside of me
take every piece of you
with you too

that way i do not have to wake
up tomorrow
just to live the rest of my life
knowing the only thing
i have left
is vacancy in my bones
and hollowness
replacing the feel of you

WHEN DUSK MEETS DAWN

just like that you were gone
and every second that passed
after your departure
i could feel myself forgetting you
and you forgetting me

we had the world in our hands
but no sense of direction
this was no *skinny love*
we were made for **something bigger**
but before you fell through
the cracks in my heart
i had already slipped out of
the spaces between your fingers

THE HOPES FOR LOVE IN
ANOTHER LIFE

brave

is a heart that can start over
that can take out the bullet
that created the wounds
is a heart that remains soft
within the eyes of love
while lust has one finger
on the trigger
whispering

come closer baby
let's turn you into a ruin

A MODERN FAIRYTALE

you offer him your heart
you expect him to say something
anything
touch it
hold it
take it to call his own
but he does not
he stands there still
as if you are something
he does not want to touch
to love
to hold
he leaves you to be a victim of *winter*
so you will spend the rest of
your life waiting for *summer*
but honey you have it all wrong

the sunshine looks nothing like his face
and you sure as hell
will not find summer in this place

SEASONS OF YOU

i have only ever seen the sunset looking into loves eyes
with you i felt a million suns burning
with you i finally watched the sunrise

it is the waiting game kind of love
the type where moments pass you by
while you sit still
frozen in thought
covered in holes
from nothing but the feel
of him
of her
burning through your veins
burning through your heart
yet you continue to wait
for you know their love
is the only thing to fill up
the spaces
the holes
the gaps
the emptiness
you hold hope that maybe
just maybe
one day you will be whole again

                that they
            will come back
            and make you
            whole again

FEUILLEMORT

i lay on this bed of roses
sheets stained with spilt love
coloured in memories
i do not know
to keep or to forget
as i lay on this bed
i begin to feel the thorns
come through

this place is no home
for these walls drip colours
that only remind me of you

MY HEART HAS BECOME
A HAUNTED HOUSE

sometimes we want
what is best for someone else
more than we want it for ourselves
we sacrifice our sanity
and trade it for their happiness
we take on their demons
just so they will not
lose the battle
even if it means we do
the most dangerous moment
is when you realize
they hold the gun pointed at your heart
and you know you would still
take that bullet
for him
for her

ALL FOR THE SAKE OF LOVE

the most damaging feeling
to be imprinted upon the soul
is having been left by love
at your worst
at your weakest

for the fight back into
your skin comes from
you wanting to be whole again
not from trying to collect all
your missing pieces

SOUL RENOVATIONS

it is only in the moment
you are about to lose something
you begin to value its presence
in that moment you find out
that love was and always
will be the answer
it is the only thing that holds us
together through the chaos
the only thing that gives us hope
that someday we will
find peace in all we lost
that someday we will find
the road that leads us back home
to them
to you

A TRAIL OF WHISPERS

it is hard to love
someone who has
a heart like an hourglass
and the hands of a magician
you cannot predict in time
when they will come
and when they will go

PART II

i made a deal with time
to only live in the past
for he promised to always
bring me back to you
he told me i would lose tomorrow
yet i still nodded my head
for the future is no place for me without

    you

A LOVER'S SACRIFICE

how do you expect to have all of me
when i was never whole to begin with
it would take your entire lifetime
to find all the missing pieces of me
from sink drains
to stained bed sheets
song lyrics and moving vehicles
i will always be scattered
i will always be lost
in the whirlwind of people
of places
who have only ever
taken from me

you will spend all your time
trying to fix me
i do not want that
you deserve a love that is whole
a love that is always on time
a heart that knows how to love back
my clocks are broken
and i am still searching for my heart
still searching for myself
all through these cities
somewhere on this scattered map

DRIVING IN REVERSE

i have added your name
to the list of people who have left
going through the names
yours is the hardest to say out loud
the hardest to draw a line across
i never did want to believe
it was over
that you were really leaving
that in a second all of you
all of us could *be gone*

weeks and months
passed on the calendar
yet my heart still stayed
in the belief that maybe
just maybe you would come back
then i realized my hands
were holding onto emptiness

i had to let you go
it was killing me knowing
i had been holding on to something
someone
that was letting go all along

DANGER ZONES

the skies beneath my midnight eyelids
bleed nostalgia
even in the depths of my subconscious
you still manage to ignite a fire
through every part of me
forever filled with
the smell of you
burning throughout
every inch of my memory

IRIDESCENT SCARS OF LOVE

when the music drowns you
in nothing but the sound of them
turn it off
when home begins to feel
like an unfamiliar chamber
the walls bleeding memories of them
paint over those walls red
when the silence starts to echo
to scream their name
plug your ears
and that moment your heart starts
to miss him
miss her
close your eyes

remember the power
they have over you
do not let them destroy you
pick up all your love
find a home for it in someone else
you have no choice
you have to

THE HEARTACHE STOPS WHEN
YOU WANT IT TO

keep close
the kind of love that
kisses the wounds of your soul
the kind of love that
feels like silk
tastes like honey
the kind of love that
touches your scars
and suddenly you feel
the light pouring
out of all your darkness
like gold

AMARANTHINE

we destruct ourselves

we set off the bomb
we let ourselves drown
it is mostly when love
is dripping from our lips
maybe it is because emotions
get the best of us
then we begin to live
underneath the clouds
of disbelief
of denial
which ends up hurting our hearts more
for that one day we wake up
and that empty hole
where they used to be is still there
suddenly you realize how you
have been fooling yourself
that you are fine
when the truth is your heart
will always have a hole
where they once lived
in that place they once called home

we destroy ourselves
because no matter
how bad we hurt
we can never let go
of the people we need to
we do not want to believe
in the word goodbye
the second it begins to drip
from our tongues
so we sit amongst the shadow of time
killing ourselves
slowly and softly to the sound
of the clock echoing
a past lover's name
and once upon a time

TRYING TO FIND THE SWITCH
TO TURN IT ALL OFF

i watched you light the match
letting your own fire die
just to keep the flames
of love
of him
burning inside of you
alive

DANCING UNDERNEATH
LIBRA'S MOON

they warned me
that there would be days like this
where you wake up
and everything looks unfamiliar
where no roads will take you home
where you find yourself laying on the
bathroom floor
and it is a fight to crawl
back into your own skin
days where your bones shake
and your ribcage caves in
for an avalanche is happening inside you
days where the memories
come back so vividly
and you try so hard to run
from your own thoughts
but you end up reading the letters
you once wrote for them
and then it starts all over again

you cannot fool yourself
that you do not
miss him
miss her
on days like this

CLEANING OUT YOUR CLOSET

they tell me to detach myself
to let go of it all
to do it for **me**
not for *him*
they tell me to take my heart
from my hands and put it back
where it belongs
to hide it
to never give it back to him
they tell me to be **strong**
that he is my *weakness*
that the only thing he has done
was break me
yet what they do not know is
how he loved me
when all the lights were off
that maybe we were not made of
sunlight in the middle of july
that maybe we were made
in the december frost
on the windows
under the moonlight
maybe we were made to have
a love trapped in the dark
for only we can see the light in it
maybe it is a type of love so rare
that no one can see it

only we
only we can feel it

ROOM 5608

i was afraid that if i kissed you
my lips would always crave you
that nobody could ever come and
replace the taste of you
i was afraid that loving you would be
the most vanquishing thing to do
i would not be able to pull the plug
turn off the switch
to ever stop

and my darling my heart
cannot afford another
addiction

STORM CHASERS

we are standing in the eye of the storm
as nostalgia fills the silence
with memories
that once brought this love together
as we spin in circles
out spills the truth
followed by the thunder of my heart
to let you know it still beats for you
that i will hold onto you
even though these winds
try to convince me otherwise
there is no force strong enough to pull
you out of my thoughts
out of my heart

i finally know what love is
what it feels like
in the moment i should have *let go*
i held on tighter
i refused to give up
to believe our love
is just a sinking ship
that we are just a tragic disaster

ANCHORS

our fear was never
falling in love

it was this
right here

falling out of it

TIDES THAT WERE ALWAYS
DOOMED TO DROWN US

you say it
like you will not be coming back
like it is the last time i will see you
the way it rolls off your tongue
falls out of your mouth
makes me think
maybe you really are leaving

you walk away
leaving me here with your ghosts
these shadows of you
these goosebumps
whispering the word
i dreaded to hear
the most from your mouth

goodbye

yet my hands plead
my heart begs
that it is only for now my love

PLEASE MEET ME IN
MY DREAMS TONIGHT

it could have been
that you were the saint
while i was the sinner
that you were
digging us out of the hole
while i made the hole in our love bigger
maybe i was the disease
and you were my only remedy

maybe all this time
i was the fire
touching your heart of
gasoline

ASHES OF LOVE

let us wipe these slates
we call our hearts clean
of all the dirt and lies
let us clean out these
closets we have full of skeletons
that only remind us of the past
of the demons
who follow us back home
let us go back
to the day we first met
and do everything over
maybe
just maybe
we can have love
this time without struggle

THE CALLING OF SPRING

my heart bleeds dry for you
all over your transparent lines
i want to resuscitate this love
and bring you back to life
sedate all your pain
breathing life into your
pulmonary veins
in hopes you'd wake up
and our love
would still be a taste
that remains

A HEART COMATOSE

you can find me hidden
in the last ray of light
the sun emits as she
is ready to fall asleep
i leave with her too

i refuse to lay under the moonlight
to only walk my dreams
looking for you

SOLAR ECLIPSE

the ink of your heart
still leaks from the tips of my fingers
as i write these secrets
upon this blank page
spilling out a galaxy of feelings
i never let surface
from my memories that still
bleed out love for you
from my veins
to only wish every time
i write of you
it would hurt a little less
and the ink of you
trapped in my pen
would eventually fade

LETTERS TO YOU

we spent so much time
chasing the lights
trying to grab our silhouette dreams
trying to find love
through the shadows on the wall
and in between hotel bed sheets
that we let each other slip
through *the only moment* that was ours

somewhere in between
running from the past
and praying for a future
of perfect synchrony

3 A.M. IN VEGAS

the moment you decided to stop loving me
tell me what it took to leave me
tell me what was it that made you let me go

what scares me is how you do not
fear my fire
these explosive bombs
hanging from the strings of my heart
these burning torches i have for hands

you still want me
you still want my love
i ask you why

you said that you would
rather be burned by my flames
than live a whole lifetime
without ever knowing my touch
the only thing that scares you
the only fear you have
is losing me
losing my love
if ever the lights go down
if ever my fires die out

INFECTIONS

we are just destroying each other
in this game of love
trying to claim ownership
of one another's hearts
while we are running around
the field with our hearts on fire
declaring war
we are lost
looking for the same love
the same answer
and the only way to win this game
is to give up this fight
to surrender
for we both know we will never
win without each other

i need you just as much
as you need me
what is love
what is war
without one another

CALLING A TRUCE

this is a time
where our hearts lay heavy in our hands
having nothing left
but a house of memories to reflect on
this is something too big to wash
down the drain
or to fit in the back of our closets

we will carry our heavy hearts
around town
everyday
every passing day until
we meet again

**PEOPLE THAT ARE
GONE TOO SOON**

my mind has slipped
into a state of amnesia
and my blurry heart
cannot seem to make out the distance
in your face anymore
you wear the mask of time
oh so convincing
for all along your eyes
fooled me with a future
not knowing your lips had already
written me off as the past

STAGES OF DENIAL

i need you to know i was always there
maybe your memory
put me in the shadows
on the back burner
or maybe you never remembered
because you were never looking
you were always looking past me

i am even standing
in front of you now
and there you are again
looking right through me

ALCOHOLISM

i left your fingerprints on my windowsill
to remind my restless heart
that you are just a world away
somewhere out there
maybe far
maybe near

it was just a minute ago
that you were with me
right here

A RAINY DAY IN
PARIS

you tell me i have changed
that the lights are not on upstairs
it looks as if nobody is home
you tell me to find myself
my way back into my own skin
you tell me i am not the same
that you miss the old me
yet this is me
without the mask
with the lights really on
this is what i look like
without you
without your love
clothing me
all the paint has washed off
you can see the stains on my body
the splinters in my heart
the cracks on my hands
you finally taste the bitterness on my lips
you are not used to the old me
you're used to the fully furnished
one-bedroom home i built for you
but that is gone
she is gone
and i would not expect
any different from you

THE ROOTS OF DEPRESSION

do not give me the promise of the world
do not give me the promise of love
til death do us part the
only promise
i beg you to say
i beg you to keep
is that you will not break me tonight

fragility trembles heavily
through my bones at night

ONLY THE MOON HEARS THE WAY
THE WOLF CRIES

when the sound of your heart
screams for resuscitation from
the nightmares
you have been having
causing your pulse to crave sedation
may you rest assured
my love will be the medication
to put you at ease
to give you salvation

INCUBATION PERIODS

aphrodite told me
she was a goddess lost on land
seeking to be set free
for mount olympus
could never be home
to a heart bound to the seas
how underwater
love was the oxygen she would breathe
yet when it came to love
above poseidon's shores
she spilled her love out
so easily

MYTHOLOGY

time handed us an hour
you only gave me a minute
your fingerprints lay under cover
though my body does not fail to exhibit
these tales of lust
you left behind so vivid
fooling yourself
telling me a love like this
a love like mine
you prohibit

THE TASTE OF NAZLANMAK

i wake up craving you
my hunger for you is overwhelming
a desire to touch your flaming heart
even though i know i will get burned
yet something about you
makes the bad feel compelling
the good feel lonely
and on a night like this

i do not want to be alone

INTO THE WILD

infatuation tells me
to keep my eyes steady
while compulsion persuades me
to feel not think
so i stumble over my thoughts
hoping not to find
a trace of desperation
that will arouse the waves
amongst this impending ocean
of obsession
for these fantasies of you
that tempt me
were never part of the plan
an unexpected intention

DRIVING THE CALIFORNIA COASTLINE

if you asked me what my middle name
was i would tell you nostalgia
for lately i have been
staring at my reflection
trying to catch a glimpse
of my own halo but it keeps
disappearing
maybe because
i have been wearing these heels of sin
walking all over town
or maybe it is because
disaster never looked so good
until i saw it on you

MIDNIGHT BLUES

you fight
more wars than your hands can take
more than your heart can take
cease fire
let me into the wreckage
alongside the gunshot wounds
i want to be the one who saves you
so let me spill love
into your pain-paralyzed veins tonight

ALLEVIATION

it takes every bone in my body
to get out of bed each morning
i have to convince myself
that the sun will beam
through these holes
love has burned through me
that i will feel light
i will feel warmth again
some days are better than others
other days i feel like the whole world
is anxiously waiting for me to crumble
yet the thunderstorms happening inside
my heart
refuse to let them
see me weak
see me cry
lightning strikes
in hopes they fear
standing underneath my stormy skies

HEART MURMURS

remember that love should
always come easy
and those who make it hard
do not deserve you
your love
your time

remember your heart
still beat before this
that heartbreak is not permanent
along with everything we feel
it is all temporary
we are temporary
the only way to move on is to remember
that time will always carry us
to different people
different places in life
give us new hearts to love and
cities to call home

HOLY GRAIL

you spoke your love for me
like the depth of the ocean
begging me to throw myself
in the serenity of your motion
to rest assured that i am swimming
in currents of your devotion
yet the rust stains on my heart prove
your love is leaking
eroding
i have swum
the depths of your heart
only to drown heavily in my own
vacant emotions

ONCE LIFELINES NOW PANIC CORDS

i have nothing more
than this sandcastle heart
hoping to survive
another day through these storms

i have nothing more
than these pens for fingertips
that tend to colour pages
with the saudade-soaked poetry
dripping from my words

i am nothing more than
a door that people walk out of
just as fast as they came in
i am nothing more than
a stranger in a crowded train station
trying to find my way
back home
maybe back *home to me*
maybe back *home to you*

THE TASTE OF LACUNA

you will never understand
the intensity of heartbreak
until the moment you watch love
fall right out of the eyes
of the person you love

your palms begin to sweat desperation
your lungs start to collapse
and your heart begins to crack
in the most destructive way
with nothing left but the weight
of a thousand memories
bleeding out of you
through every shade of your being
through every inch of your bones

GRAVEYARDS

it is only in the moment we are
about to lose something we
realize how hard it is to let go

we realize time only ever
wanted the best for us
yet we were so busy carrying around
our heavy hearts of oblivion
that the words fell right through
the cracks in our teeth
left to swallow the god-awful truth
that the only reason we are holding on
is the fear of what will creep
into the empty space
the second it leaves us
the second it is gone
the *second they are gone*

MONSTERS UNDER THE BED

we are all trying
to find our way back
to someone
to a place
to a moment
we once existed in
that breathed purpose in our lungs
that lit a fire in our hearts
that made us feel something
worth remembering
we get lost in the crave
of trying to find our way back to it
trying to hold on to it
of wanting it endlessly
over and over
and over again

THE HANDS OF GREED

i get you have this burning desire
under your feet to always run
this uncontrollable itch upon your palms
as if you are longing for something
this addiction to showering
just to wash off the dirt on your skin
from those who have
only coloured you in
shades of grey
how you have only ever
tasted pain in love
living under skies of loss and heartache

now what defines you
is your ability to overcome it all
fighting to see the light
even in your darkest hour
and loneliest night

BAND-AIDS ON FISTS THAT
BLEED SALVATION

do you remember
how love first tasted
when it touched your tongue
the wildfire it ignited
as it was reaching
the pit of your soul
yet you let the fire die out
the feelings fade away
years have passed and i bet you are
sitting there thinking you can
find the same taste of
love
inside the mouth of someone else

you are only fooling yourself
eating that bowl of heartache
and deception for breakfast

7 A.M. TABLE TALK

promise me

if our days ever become numbered
that we will spend our last
few seconds together
close
making love to our shadows
so when you are gone
and the nights grow lonely
i can still feel you
by making drunken love
to your
ghosts

I BEG TO BE HAUNTED BY YOU
FOR AN ETERNITY

he wondered where
she put it all
the graveyard of her past
the clouds of her emotions
the ocean of love she bled
every night across the floor

until he saw her
through the crack of a shadow
beating her heart
just to stain her pages
with poetry-poisoned words

POETRY WAS MADE TO BE BOTH
TRAGIC AND BEAUTIFUL

i miss us
i miss our love
before you started
to taste like a stranger
i miss the fire
we became along the way
and all of those late nights
our hearts reeked
of gasoline and danger

TIME BOMBS

if my pillowcase didn't still smell like you
maybe i wouldn't dream of you the way i still do

we throw up our fists
against the hands of destruction
blaming the winds for our demise
for our faith facing love's abduction
yet the lightning bolts of chaos
strike us with eruption
so our hearts can remember
sometimes we need a disaster
to destroy our weaknesses
for freedom only lies
within the face of
reconstruction

EVEN THE ROMAN WALLS
WERE BUILT TO FALL

can you hear that
the sound of the ocean settling
after a roaring storm
do you see that
the sun waking to kiss the lips
of the moonlit shore

we are all cursed with darkness
we are all cursed with disaster
just like the ocean
forgives the storm
just like the sun
still loves the moon
we are here to stay
to find love
despite the winds screaming run
you are doomed
you are doomed

BREATHING WOUNDS

it was never love who was the wolf

it was lust
baby how could you not see
his teeth growling
or hear him
howling to the moon

there goes another one
there goes another one

these wolves
you have been running with
do not see you
as something to love
they see fragility dripping
from your heart
you are something to hunt
you are something to devour
you are just another kill
they will say anything
to get into you
to taste the velvet running
underneath your skin

ANIMAL KINGDOM

tell me
tell me
to love him
to love her
more than your own flesh
more than your own bones
is that selfless love
or is that just *reckless*

THE CONDITIONS OF
UNCONDITIONAL LOVE

how oh how
did we become so reckless
saying we love
we admire the warmth of the sun
yet abandon the face and light
of the moon

how oh how
did we end up here
allowing ourselves to carry around
these heavy hearts
these numb hands
afraid to touch the depth of love

how oh how
did we mistake one another for
strangers fearing what is to happen
what is to come
the second we let someone in
the second we fall in love

we share the same earth
we fall asleep under the same sky
we are visitors here
the healing power of human connection
is the most important weapon
we all carry inside

FLOWERS OF ANCESTRY

i have run out of so many things like
patience
expectations

yet i have never
run out of desire
to turn you into poetry
that is the only thing
i am certain
my heart will always crave
my hands will always remember to do

COFFEE STAINS

they say love is magic

yet what they fail to tell you
the fallout
the coming undone
the split within the seams of it
my god
is it ever bloody tragic

EVEN THE ROSE IS BOUND
TO THE THORN

this is heartache
this is torture
this is pain
sitting underneath the sky
as he cries

i am sorry
i am sorry

that you spent all your love
wishing on shooting stars
to only have them burn out
to only have everything
you have ever wanted
leave you behind

i am sorry
i am sorry

that the moon howled
nothing but the word goodbye
and love was your heart's reason
for suicide

AN ETERNITY OF
BURNING

he asked me who
i wrote about

i turned around
ripping open the cracks in my heart
and said

i am tearing open these wounds
so you can see the depths
i have loved you
look closer
underneath all the words
can you see they are covered in you

poetry poetry poetry
i bleed all of this for you

NEPENTHE

the bruises
the blood
the aching
the pain
the wreckage we became

i never knew love
could come like this
i never knew love
could leave like this
demanding us to hold
our bleeding hearts in our hands
with nothing left
but to feel hurt
like this

STITCHES THAT KEEP
COMING UNDONE

i cannot find the strength
the will
to wipe your fingerprints
from my bedroom window
or forget the way you wrote
i love you
in the frost of the past fog
a part of me still needs to see it
to remind my heart
love is infinite
it is the hourglass
which makes it a temporary stay
everything you love
has an expiration date

when the hands of time
came looking for you
knocking know
i cried
i ached
for the parts of you taken away
yet there was and still is
pieces of you i loved so deeply
no amount of time could ever
take those memories of
loving you
away

LOVE WROTE ME OFF
AS SKIN AND BONES

i lie awake
burning in desire underneath
the light of the moon
aflame with the thought of
how much i want you

(how much i need you)

19

i have watched you scream relentlessly
to the heavens
i have watched the stars you once wished upon
explode inside of you
i have watched the way love crumbles you
yet fixes you all in the same instant
you have questioned
you have cut yourself open
you have planted gravestones all over
your wounds
you have wrapped caution tape all over
your heart
you fear love is just another word for *vacancy*
all you can remember is
how love left you
drowning within the same oceans
that once told you
not to be afraid to dive deeper
to swim further
you have let the hands of grief
turn off the lights of hope inside you
time has become the enemy
for every second you have to live without
all that you have lost

the scars only show you how
you will carry around this pain forever

but i promise you this
you won't

in the same way your wounds
ache and bleed
they also heal
the light will find you
when the sun rises again
your heart will wake up and without you
even knowing
it is still going to beat for you
your lungs will find new ways to breathe
time will bring the hands of love
back to you
they will knock
on the doors of your heart
they will hold you
they will teach you
even though you have
loved and lost
you will love again
and again

YOU WILL ALWAYS LOVE AGAIN

you carried my heart
across the starlit sky
to the knees of july's sunrise
just to show my soul
some days i will wear the sun
ferociously *wanting to burn*
other days i will wear the moon
tucked away *wanting to hide*

   both are perfectly fine

GROWING UP
WITH ANXIETY

my recovery began
the second my heart found
forgiveness
buried underneath centuries
of blame

I AM TIRED OF HURTING

the hurt no longer
wakes me in the middle of the night
i have accepted your absence
i have learned to live with the nightmares
i no longer keep the door unlocked
after years of realizing
you are never coming back

this is me finally
healing
closing the curtains blowing
all the lights out finally
locking the door

letting you go
was the homecoming
of my soul

THE SACRIFICE

can you not see the way your heart
grows a tongue to lick away
the catastrophe
seeping from your wounds
whether you are aware or oblivious
you are always healing
inside of your soul exists a whole galaxy
stitched of whimsical constellations
that have spent thousands of years
trying to teach you

these scars
are your destiny
these scars
are your body's stars

IF YOU EVER NEED
A REASON TO STAY

chapter one

was so promising
i finally started to live
for the sunrise and not for the sunset
for i knew it would bring me you
i had so much hope for the future
when i met you
i finally felt the holes in my heart
closing
healing

i always wanted nothing more than
to feel love
not bleed love
with you i did
with you i believed
i was capable of loving
i was the person i always wanted to be
i was me

chapter two

was so enigmatic
you became distant
out of touch
out of reach
i started to fall in love
with the sunset again
i did not want to be awake
to only miss you
to only sit with my thoughts
waiting for you
all i wanted was for you
to be there
to be here

i realized in those moments
a love that only sees the light
is rare
i became the sun
you became the moon
stuck
trying to chase your love
catch your light
find my way back home
to you

chapter three

was a feeling i knew all too well
a feeling i never thought
would come from loving you

a b a n d o n m e n t

i looked for you in everything
you were nowhere to be found
i waited until the blood in my heart dried
and your love became the air suffocating me
i did not want to be awake
to feel your absence
i did not want to close my eyes
to only dream of your presence
ever since chapter three
nothing has been the same
i have not been the same
i fear i will never be the same

chapter four

this is vacancy

my heart has become a
vacant hotel room
waiting for you
waiting for love
waiting for your occupancy

HIDEAWAY

if desire is enough to kill you
then let me die the most
elysian
euphoric death
at the hands of him
my lover
my muse
burning ferociously
engulfed in flames of passion
dancing one last time
through the skyline of love
before the sun of him
sets
inside my soul

i want the world to see
i sacrificed myself for love
all to give birth
to these words right now
that you read

THE FIRE OF DESIRE

i walked through the doors of this love
with one thing on my mind
a forever state of mind

AQUARIUS
you have torn apart the seam of your
heart trying to find the exit sign out
you bathe yourself in destruction
you rebel against religion
yet your pores spill out nothing but sin
when will you come back home
into your skin
and make peace with those demons
you built within

PISCES
you were never told how much light is
buried deep within you
so you spent years trying
to swallow the sun
when will you give up
your fear of the fire
grab the stars
set the sky on fire
let the world watch you burn
you never needed them to tell you you
are the light
can't you see it
can't you feel it
pouring
flowing
exploding
out from the universe beneath your skin

ARIES

you carry around war
like it is the only thing your hands
know how to hold
yet the holes you cut through your skin
only show how badly you want to heal
so you can finally feel whole
when will you bandage the damage
so your bleeding heart can finally love
before the world traded you loathe
for your soul

TAURUS

you dug a grave for every part of you
that died the day love left you
you arranged your own funeral
the day you watched them all walk away
when will you stop carving the word
abandonment
in your bones
when will you finally free your soul
plant flowers in your lungs
so you can breathe again
and finally let all of this hurt go

GEMINI

you are in constant battle with yourself
yet you fool them into believing
the world is to blame
for all of this disaster cursed your way
when will you accept that you are both
the god
the monster
stop running and take off the mask
there are plenty of reasons to love again
and even more reasons to stay

LEO

you carry more light inside of your eyes
than any sun i have ever seen dancing
across the sky in the middle of july
when will you awaken and realize
all of these roses are here because
you birthed them in the soil of your soul
when will you start dancing again who
cares what they think
grab the skin of your dreams
flourish
glow
grow

LIBRA
you fill your days with the word busy
in all the ways you are so afraid
of who you are when you are all alone
when will you stop feeding yourself
with the blood of lust
at the hands of your own addictions
when will you admit
the inside of your heart cries the loudest
for love is what you ache for
the most

LETTERS TO THE WOMEN WITHIN ME

to the souls
who beat their hearts
who bleed themselves dry
who kill themselves over
and over
all for the love of art

may your fire forever
burn alive

DEEPLY ROOTED

this is the end of the road
the start of a new beginning
the moment where the war
is over and you are waving your flag
to show you have won
this is the part where
everything you built is gone
so you could find your hope
is still the soil you stand upon
this is the last breath you will take
before you discover
a new way to breathe
a new way to live
this is all happening
to heal the burns from the fire
the wounds from the war
this is your resurrection
your taste of redemption
the day you cease fire
for disaster
can no longer kiss your lips
your heart
is not a battlefield anymore
you found yourself through the smoke now
may you rise from your ashes
for you have never been more free
than in this moment
do you feel alive
this is the moment you finally have wings
reborn
ready to fly

XXVIII MMXV

ACKNOWLEDGMENTS

To **God,** thank you for igniting a fire inside me with the gift of writing. You have showed me that with this life you have given me, my story, I can heal not only my own wounds, but those who have the same wars tearing apart their bones.

To my best friend **Valerie Dayrit,** thank you for breathing love and faith into my soul. My brightest day would never exist if you were not there in my darkest hour. Everything I do, *forever,* is for you.

To my sister **Josie MacLeod,** thank you for fighting these wars with me. Your spirit illuminates this shaded world, and I will spend the rest of my life chasing the light with you.

To my father and guardian angel **John MacLeod,** thank you for leaving behind your undeniable strength within me. I wish for nothing more than for you to be looking down upon me, proud. I love you.

To **him,** thank you for filling my veins with euphoria. You will always be my desire; my muse.

dear survivors

these bodies we rent from the gods
were created to expire
the hands of time we borrow from the universe
one day we will have to retire
every morning you get to wake
beneath the glowing sun *is a gift*
every night you get to come home
to the people you love *is a blessing*
spend your time here on earth
filling your lungs with compassion
sewing your scars with forgiveness
colouring your life with the fire of passion
live every moment you have with purpose
if it does not make you feel alive
if it does not make you a better human
if it does not fill your soul with light
then it is not worth your time

spend the *1,440* minutes
you have today falling in love
with the soul beneath your skin
with the flames of passion that burn inside
with the people who make you
feel most alive

with love,

    haley

        instagram: @haleymacleod
        website: hmpoetry.com

Made in the USA
Lexington, KY
05 July 2018